The Secret to Opening Your Emerging Mind

Awake, Activate, Authenticate
A Proven Action Plan for a New Era

Dr. J.F. Caputo, Ph.D.
www.DrJake.com

First published by Dog Ear Publishing
4010 W. 86th Street, Ste H
Indianapolis, IN 46268
www.dogearpublishing.net

dog ear
PUBLISHING

ISBN: 978-160844-623-0

This book is printed on acid-free paper.

Printed in the United States of America

INTRODUCTION

It has been said; ***"everyone has a book in them."*** I have been told more than once that I should write a book. I didn't think I had the knowledge, skill or desire to write. Having written more than one thesis and a dissertation for my Ph.D. in Metaphysical Parapsychology, I came to realize that writing a book should not be much different.

The inspired passages in this book came to me one at a time. Each morning, based on my predominant state of mind, what was going on in my life and how I felt emotionally, I would be inspired to write something. I would then post the passage online. Each passage you see reflects aspects of my life over an extended period of time.

Sometimes I read a passage that I penned and it looks new, as I do not recall writing it. Many were written in the wee early hours of day when I was not totally awake.

Each of us is capable of amazing things when we open our minds to listen to our hearts and souls speak the truth. I am grateful that many people on social networking sites find value and comfort in my words. It is my sincerest desire that you find value and comfort in my words also.

Dr. J.F. Caputo, Ph.D.

Chicago, June 2010

How to Use This Book Most Effectively

We are entering a ***new era*** never before imaginable. This era is already emerging and calls for humanity to evolve in ways that may seem unconventional. History shows that we have been forceful in most pursuits. The ***new era*** calls for us to live from an empowered, compassionate, loving state of being, with peace and cooperation prevailing.

The Secret to Opening Your Emerging Mind is a collection of my personal philosophies, lessons I have learned and inspirational words that ***just came to me***.

These daily passages inspire powerful action. The passages call out to you to take immediate action. Many things are shifting in the ***new era*** and will challenge old behavior. Inspired actions that emerge from the passages will make the ***new era*** transition less challenging. This new way of relating to our world is revealing new opportunities.

Allow Your Destiny to Unfold

I want you to get the utmost value out of this book as it functions differently than other books. It is most effective when read according to the following guidelines.

For Maximum Results (Recommended)

Skim the pages like fanning a deck of cards. Stop wherever it feels right. Before you open the book, ask; ***"left page or right page?"*** When you get your answer, for example say left; you open your book to the left page of your stopping point. Whatever passage you see first is your passage for the day. This passage is your call to action.

The beauty is this; there is no predetermined place for you to stop. You stop when it feels right to you. You are putting yourself in alignment with The Universe by going with the flow of life. You are shaping your own destiny.

Once you read your daily passage go to the section "***My Emergence Journal***" that begins in the middle of the book. Note the page number and date of the passage you are referring to. Your first Journal entry may look like this; 33-4 July 4, 20XX. You jot down what you are doing to allow the words to inspire you to action. Every day that you read a passage, write in your Journal also.

As you write in your journal you will see a progressive shift in the way your mind is evolving. You will also experience a sense of well being in a totally new way. ***"Trust the process and allow things to unfold."***

For Results Based on Specific Topics

If you want to read about specific topics, let's say ***relationships;*** go to the back of your book to the section titled ***Topic References***. Look under ***relationships*** and you will find every page that has a passage that is related to relationships. You may read this book like any other book by starting on page one and progressing forward. Using your book in this manner will give you many things to ponder and may possibly be overwhelming.

May these passages reveal a world within you that inspires change in the world around you! Best Regards, Dr. Jake.

Dedication

This book is dedicated to my Guiding Source I call God and my two little angels, Layla Rey and Evangeline Rey. I also dedicate this book to the memory of my big brother, Richard A. Caputo and the many supporters who always encourage my writing, teach me love, and support my ongoing work.

Many situations in life call for extraordinary measures. The most important situations often call for more than thinking, they require us to analyze how we ***feel***. Our emotional feelings let us know if we are in alignment with ***Divine*** flow, or if we are being resistant.

What you ***perceive is what you*** tend to ***believe***. You can change your beliefs if you align your mind with your heart and soul. It's just a matter of trusting the process.

Many people are in love with the idea of marriage, but ***not*** in love with a specific person. Some are in love with the concept of love and ***not*** a lover. Always be open to love, by being loving. If you are a loving person, you will love and appreciate yourself. Appreciating and loving one's self naturally attracts others that resonate with our healthy self love. To thy own self be true, and attract love to ***you.***

Your perception of the world gets shaped by the vibration that radiates outward from you. This has been known for a long time but, often misunderstood. The key is to take responsibility for ***everything*** that happens in your life. If you knowingly take responsibility for creating what ***is***, you will become more aware of this phenomenon and create what you desire with ***intention*** that is much clearer.

There are three things about which you can be hundred percent certain. 1) You choose who you care about. 2) People, things and circumstances are constantly changing. 3) Only you know how you feel about any given situation (mad, glad, happy, sad, etc.). We may not totally understand why we feel a certain way but we always know how we feel. Find the good in ***all that is.***

The more we experience and acknowledge that everything is intertwined the more connected we feel to ***all that is***. The more connected we feel, the more grateful we become.

Each of us has our own perception of reality based on what we believe to be true. Many people and many traditions look to influence what they would like others to believe. What you ***experience, feel, and know,*** exceeds any belief.

It has been said, ***love*** is an action word. When we truly love someone; we think it, say it, and show it. When we are expressing it all three ways, we are truly ***being love***. When we are being it, we see it, when we are being and seeing it, we feel it. Understanding our feelings is a stepping stone toward self love and self mastery.

If a plan is not in place, failure ***may*** be forthcoming. If you have not intentionally created a pathway to your desires, you will be working with random energies. ***The Universe*** says: ***OK!*** You bring about that which you intentionally think, feel and have gratitude for. You also bring about that which you act upon. Starting now be aware of what you allow into your conscience.

The words you use, spoken or thought, are a direct representation of what you believe about your world. Consciously choose your words and be mindful of their meanings. You will find that your new vocabulary will be a source of inspiration.

As long as we function as ***physical beings*** we are subject to physical laws of nature, including polarity or duality. Examples are; peace/war, good/bad and feast/famine. We have the capacity to transcend our physical limitations by embracing our ***Divine consciousness*** that is pure love, void of duality. Live as a physical being or live as a ***spiritual*** being, the choice is ***yours.***

Love resonates as the highest vibration in ***The Universe***. Be love and you will see love.

I plan to do that someday, or, when I have the time, I am going to write a book. We have all said and heard things like that many times. The message is simple. If you want to write a book ***be*** an author. ***Do*** what authors ***do.*** If you are not going to ***be*** whatever it is stop talking about it and let it go. Keep thoughts and words that inspire action.

Everything that happens in life can be viewed as good or disappointing. Even the most disappointing experience brings seeds of value or wisdom. It all depends on how we choose to perceive the experience. Look for the blessings in all things and you will find them. When you do give gratitude, more will naturally follow.

The common dictionary definition of ***respect*** is: to hold in esteem or to honor. Generally speaking most people who are honored or held in high esteem have earned respect based on something that they have done or something that they do. If we strive to treat everyone with respect, we will ultimately learn to love and respect ourselves at a higher level, thus allowing us to love others at a higher level.

Thoughts come and go. Some are conscious and some are subconscious. Ultimately, thoughts become the words we speak and a revelation to the world of our values. Keeping your word shows that you are accountable. ***Being*** your word shows that you are ***Divine.***

Your happiness is hundred percent your responsibility. Being that you know this to be true, examine this aspect of your life. If you have given away any authority over your body, mind, or soul, today is the day to begin life anew. Use ***Intention*** and ***action*** to take responsibility for your life, demonstrating that you are your own authority.

Sometimes we unexpectedly learn something from one area of our life that can be applied to another area of our life. This usually happens when there are parallel states of emotion, as one situation triggers the other. It's like a two for one sale if we realize the parallel connection.

The ***body***, ***mind***, and ***soul*** each have their own fields of intelligence. They are one with ***the field*** that scientists call the overall field of intelligence. When the ***triune man*** (***body, mind, soul***) is consciously connected to ***the field*** and has dreams, ideas, and visions; what is probable is transcended into what is ***possible***. In the realm of ***The Divine*** all things are possible.

In matters of business, finance and science it is appropriate to use logic to reach conclusions. In matters of personal relationships look to your heart, as it speaks the desires of your soul. Your soul expresses desire on a physical level through the ***emotions*** of the heart. Your soul knows.

Sometimes we believe that an event needs to occur or a certain person needs to show up before we can take action. Your life is ***now***, your future is ***now*** and everything is ***now***. Work with what you have from where you are. Waiting for things to happen is coming from a place of lack and fear. You have the power ***within yourself*** to begin living your dreams now. ***Be it, see it, and love it, Now.***

If you go to a sporting event and sit on the side lines, you are a spectator not a participant. Your life is ***your*** event. If you find yourself on the sidelines of ***your*** event; you have allowed someone to take your place. You are the star of your show. Allow yourself to shine.

We attract our experiences in present time. We do this best when we engage co-creation using ***deliberate intention***. Once a clear ***intention*** is set, we see it ***as so*** and maintain a state of gratitude. We are often given signs or clues that the process ***is*** unfolding. Today, look for clues, signs, or hints that your desires are in process. The signs are all around you. Starting now, become more observant.

Children see the world as though anything is possible, because it ***is***. Your world ***is*** a reflection of what you see as possible based on how you have been conditioned. ***Now*** is the time to expand what is, ***unconditionally***.

Life presents challenges and opportunities. Some people's challenges are not easily detectable. The greatest teachers have always stressed ***being compassionate***. If someone is having an issue, don't judge, ***reach out compassionately***.

When contemplating what you ***intend*** to attract into your life, what is your ***Intention*** based upon? If it is lack, neediness, infatuation or egotism, the foundation of the ***Intention*** might be on shaky ground. If your ***Intention*** is based on ***love***, ***service*** or ***purpose*** you are in ***expansion.*** This is in alignment with the way ***The Universe*** works.

Studies show that the first sixty minutes upon waking and the last sixty minutes before bed shape your day. Be conscious of what you think, say and do during these two periods of time. You will shift into a more powerful day.

Knowledge is gained through education and experience. ***Wisdom*** is gained solely through experience. One's knowledge may be questionable, while ***wisdom*** speaks for itself and resonates with those who are open to the ***truth***.

Being and becoming boils down to potential. Each of us is born with potential like power stored in a battery. An acorn grows into ***becoming*** a tall oak tree. The acorn always had the potential of becoming an oak tree. Becoming is ***being*** that which you are capable of growing into. Intentionally utilizing your own co-creative power to create from within and become more of who you already are.

A baby cries for milk. ***When*** is the best time to feed the baby? If a man was stranded and had to walk six miles to safety, ***when*** would he choose to accept a ride? A man who led a wonderful life lies on his death bed. Somehow he is miraculously given a choice to pass on or live. ***When*** would he make that choice? You have the option of living a life you dread or design. ***When*** will you decide?

Love on any level requires; energy, caring, consideration and so on. The opposite of love is not hate; hate is the ugly side of love. Indifference is the opposite of love. Indifference is not caring, being unconcerned and does not require any energy. It is noble to show love toward all with no expectations. In all relationships it is vital to recognize that love ***is an energy exchange.***

Gandhi taught us that; the most effective way to make a difference is to ***be the difference?***

Things are not always as they appear to be in the physical world. Rather than rely on outside sources for clarification it is wiser to be one's own counsel. Base your perceptions on how things ***feel*** within, using ***Divine*** sense of intuition.

What you believe is what you receive. Whatever you believe about yourself and your world is what your mind interprets as fact. Your body takes information from your mind and inserts it into your cellular system. Shift into a state of ***being*** that is supportive of your beliefs and dreams. Act accordingly from that state of being and ***create***.

Allow all things good to happen ***through*** you so others may also be blessed by your good fortune.

Many of us are caught up in instant gratification from fast food to fast relationships. Few people are building anything of substance. That can all shift with each of us; being genuine, true to our individual values and living a life of love. Be supportive in a co-operative spirit of caring. Competition is for sports; co-operation is for living.

Sometimes we seek confirmation from others; that our ideas, plans, or choices are ***ok***. The truth is; we have it within ourselves to make wise decisions, as the Kingdom of Heaven is ***within***. You know yourself better than anyone.

All situations that require a considerable amount of thought will ultimately boil down to making ***one single decision,*** whatever that is. The ***Divine*** within will guide your decisions if you choose to listen. Choose wisely.

Every occurrence in life has upside value. One must only view it from a perspective that allows the highest good to be a consideration in the realm of possibilities.

You can hire a personal trainer but you can't buy health. You can pay for a session with a psychologist but you can't buy piece of mind. You can buy an object that supposedly has spiritual significance but you cannot buy ***soul***. You can choose to ***be*** enlightened, ***do*** whatever it takes and choose to ***have*** a conscious connection to Divinity. Just be ***it and see it.***

The Secret and other books and movies have emerged in recent years. Most people have heard, "***what you resist persists***." The explanation is critical. If we are resistant we are in a state of mind that is not allowing flow. The resistance we maintain keeps things clogged like a drain, therefore the resistance persists.

If we view obstacles as opportunities, life will be better. All it takes is a change in how we choose to see things.

Each of us is an expression of ***The Divine***, thus we are ***Divine***. The ***Divine*** is love, therefore we are love. ***Be*** the love and ***be*** responsible for creating your own joy.

The outer world is a mirror of our inner world. Do you see the real you in the mirror? ***Or*** do you see ***through*** the glass and only see others living life, thereby negating yourself? ***Be*** you and ***see*** you.

Everyone has one or more special quality, product, service or message to share with the world. If we choose to discover our special qualities we can make life better. Share it freely and ***envision*** what our world ***could*** be.

Some people work very hard to live up to someone else's expectations. For some, being genuine has gone by the wayside. Genuinely ***be*** who you are and ***be*** yourself in an honest manner. You are unique. There is no one like ***you***. Celebrate ***you*** by giving of ***yourself.***

Sometimes people are in our lives for a short while, then they leave or we leave. One person may outgrow the other or the connection might not feel like it fits for them, or for us. This is a ***no foul, no harm*** situation, no one is at fault. It is simply a matter of things not fitting. If it fits, wear it, if it doesn't fit, bless it and ***allow*** it to be.

Everyone has potential waiting to be tapped. This is a fact. Your potential is activated when your heartfelt desires are crystal clear. If you can literally taste your desires, you are expressing passion. ***Be one*** with your dreams (desires), then your dreams automatically become your reality.

It's not ***what*** you have in your life that makes a difference; it's ***who*** you have in your life. The quality of your life is directly proportionate to the quality of your relationships.

Whatever you believe you deserve has an effect on what you experience. ***Choose*** a belief that ***feels*** awesome and amazing then shift into your ***chosen*** destiny.

Faith is defined as ***belief without proof***. The more heart-felt ***faith*** you have, the more proof will appear. ***Feel faith;*** you will know when it's true.

To love yourself means: to take care of, nurture and appreciate ***you***, exactly ***as you are now***. Once you begin loving yourself you will be better able to love, take care of, nurture and appreciate others.

Being present ***within*** creates awareness to realize and ***be*** grateful that you are never without.

Many of us get caught up in everyday living, putting off things that need to be done. Before you can ***do*** anything, you must ***be***. ***Being*** requires having a vision or a dream. You must ***be it*** first from within. Then you will ***do*** whatever it takes. ***Be it*** and ***do*** the next thing that arises. View obstacles as opportunities and ***do*** one by one.

We walk through life observing and experiencing. Some people judge everything while others make discernments when needed. There is a difference. Discernment is using insight to determine if something or someone fits into a given situation. Judgment is like rendering a prison sentence. Being judgmental is an ego-minded, fear based, reactive way of living. Only ***you*** discern and choose how you view your world. Discern wisely.

It was once thought the sun rose out of the ocean. Obviously, that was found to be false. Is it possible that you, I and everyone holds onto beliefs about our own potential that are also false? Remember, the world you experience functions based on ***your*** beliefs. Do you hold onto beliefs that no longer serve you? Mind can move matter. Believe you can, and you ***will*** move mountains.

Be ***on purpose*** because you are passionate about a certain something. Allow yourself to live purposefully in a calling that drives you to go beyond your personal self and beyond your earthly lifetime. Purpose is not a popularity contest.

Being loving people, we attract loving people. This is the most fulfilling state of ***being***. From this state of ***being,*** the most effective actions of ***doing*** come forth. ***Being*** and ***doing*** allows us to ***have*** whatever our heart desires. The sequence of ***be***, ***do*** and ***have*** must be in proper order. Love must also accompany this order, as this sequence is in ***Divine*** alignment with ***The Universe***.

Some people ***think*** about making the world a better place. Some ***talk*** about it and some actually ***walk their talk*** and ***be*** the change they seek. Throughout history the most effective teachers showed us by example to: ***be it*** and ***see it***. All transformation begins from ***within***.

Each of us comes into this world as ***pure potential***. Think of yourself as a battery. Nothing happens in the circuit until the battery (containing potential to give forth energy) is installed. You already ***are*** that power. ***Just Be it.***

As we move through life, nothing is as important as the choices we make ***now!*** Why? ***Now*** is all there really ***is.***

Stop attempting to become who you ***think*** you ought to be. Let go of who you ***believe*** you must become. What remains is who you are already ***being. You are unique***.

The direction of flowing current matters not. What matters is that flow is the graceful movement of energy. Are you going with the flow of life, or fighting the flow and just getting tired? Everything is a choice. ***Go with the flow***.

The world you experience is like a gigantic mirror. It gives you exactly what you give ***it***. Do you enjoy what you are getting? If yes, give more and enjoy more. Appreciate who you ***are*** at all times. You are as perfect as you need to be. You are ***Divine***, just ***be it, see it,*** **love** ***it, live it, give it.***

Nothing stays the same. Life unfolds one moment at a time, thus, there is evolution. ***Now*** is all there is and ***this now*** has its own unique possibilities. Through ***growth and change*** is how we stay connected to ***now***. Love ***now*** for what it is and love ***you*** for who you are ***now.***

Science proves that our perceptions and perspectives shape the way we experience life. If you want ***any*** aspect of life to change, ***you*** must make a change ***first. Be it*** and ***see it.***

Being yourself is the greatest gift you have to give the world. It only requires ***three*** things on your part; the conscious awareness to listen to the desires of your heart/soul, the courage to live true to your values and the strength to release the urge to conform to the norm.

Am I responsible for everything in my life? Many things are not directly our fault but as individuals we are responsible for the clean-up. If I attract things into my life; am I attracting by default when I am not consciously aware? Only you can make this determination. Allow life to happen ***through*** you, not ***to*** you, as you are ***not*** a victim.

Believe it or not, your day is determined by you. People, situations, and circumstances show up as they may. Regardless who shows up, it's all about how you ***choose*** to respond. Go beyond reaction all the way to ***intentional response***. ***Decide*** which way you ***respond*** and you will have days that keep feeling better and better.

You must know ***yourself*** to know another. You must love ***yourself*** to love another. Above all, you must ***be*** yourself to ***be*** genuine with another person.

Each of us manifests the world that we experience, whether it be conscious or sub-consciously. When we begin to ***consciously*** manifest our world we are co-creating with ***The Divine***. ***How*** it comes to be and all the details relating to ***how*** are left to ***the Divine*** architect.

Some people say "***God helps those that help themselves.***" If I were helping myself, would ***God*** really be needed? As I develop understanding about ***The Universe*** and its **Creator** I realize that I ***am one*** with this ***Universe***. If I choose to go it alone I run on self will and could miss out on the grandest of joint ventures. If I am open to ***Divine*** wisdom my possibilities are unlimited. ***I dream big.***

Everyone has reasons for doing what they do. That does not mean that their reasons have inappropriate motives. You deserve fulfillment, happiness and joy. Choose empowering reasons for doing things that make ***you*** feel good. This will correspondingly attract people of like mind that enhance your life. The late Earl Nightingale said it best: ***"if it's to be, let it begin with me."***

Our Universe functions on love. Love ***The Source*** that created you and it becomes easy to love yourself. Love yourself as you presently are. Allow love to flow freely to all. You will attract people who mirror who you ***are***. The more you love yourself, the more love you will receive.

What you believe is what shapes your reality and the way you experience life. Absolute universal truths show a truer picture of what is real. Embrace beliefs that are in alignment with universal truths and you will be co-creating reality with the most powerful energy of ***The Universe***.

The quality of your life is a direct reflection of the quality of the conversations you have with ***The Universe***. Ask a simple question, you get a simple answer. Ask meaningful, deep, well thought-out questions, you will be guided via ***signs*** to your answer. Apply this to your life and ***The Universe*** will respond. You are never alone.

Respect people for the values they hold. This is more important than respecting them for their status or position. Values and virtues shape our personal character.

The ***present is the eternal now***. ***Past*** and ***future*** are concepts that do not exist in ***the now.***

Follow your heart's desire with certainty, as your heart is the physical counter-part to your soul. Your heart knows passionate truth. Follow your passion and truth seeks ***you.***

Words have power because ***we*** attach meaning and intention to them. ***Consciously*** choosing words that express your values allows you to authentically ***be true to thyself.***

Priorities are best kept when they are ***in order***. Sometimes order escapes the most rigid intentions. Small actions help put priorities in order. ***Intentional*** action is most powerful.

Today is a day for stillness, allowing ***The Universe*** to reveal answers and solutions to those things that are otherwise puzzling. Be still and know that you are not alone.

Our physical ***Universe*** is all about ***balance***. For every up, there is a down. The ***downs*** in life inspire us to create some of our most magnificent ***ups***. Love the down as well as the up, both are elements of growth.

The best way to insure that a recipe tastes good is to put in the proper ingredients. The way to insure that you enjoy life is to put in the proper ingredients. ***Be*** clear as to what you are attracting with proper ***Intention*** and co-create life with ***The Divine*** to suit ***your*** taste.

In life we cross bridges. Some bridges once crossed have served their purpose. Crossing back over we ***re-experience*** what we left on the other side. This may poorly serve us. Bridges that connect the heart are to be maintained in perfect order, as this serves us well.

Life ***is*** unfolding perfectly. Our plans don't always unfold quite as perfectly. ***The lesson is, love what Is, now.***

It cannot be stressed enough that; energy flows where focus goes. Meaning; whatever we focus our attention on (intentional or unintentional) is where we are sending our energy. What we focus on is what we attract into our lives. Be ***Intentionally*** clear about who, what and where you give your attention, that is the shortest distance between you and your desires.

Have you noticed people say "***have a nice day***" as they are on their way out the door? Everyone says it but few people even think about the words they speak. Challenge yourself today. Say something meaningful to those you encounter and truly mean it. It will not only be an honest gesture on your part, it will have ***substance***.

Now is ***this*** present moment. The past ***represents*** a previous now that no longer exists, except in the mind. The future ***represents*** a now that can only be pondered, as it does not exist. Therefore; this very moment is ***the only now that exists*** and is therefore the most precious. Show love by allowing others to ***be*** in your now, ***now.***

There is an immediate remedy for harnessing the power of gratitude. Carefully look around when you are out and about. In the smallest of crowds you will still see someone less fortunate than you. The moment you spot that person, ***that's your gratitude wake up call***. After you spot ***that*** person reflect upon what you are grateful for.

Some people can fit into any situation because of their love of people and wanting them to feel comfortable. They are not necessarily chameleons. However, many other people are chameleons as they do not embrace their unique ***God*** given self. If you fear being the true ***you***, the world is deprived of your unique gifts.

Whatever you believe you deserve has an effect on what you experience in life. ***Choose*** a belief that ***feels*** awesome and amazing and shift into your ***chosen*** destiny.

Faith is defined as ***belief without proof***. The more heartfelt ***faith*** you have the more proof appears anyway. ***Keep faith in what comforts you best.***

The mind thinks, chooses what to believe and knows facts. ***True knowing*** is the realm of the ***Divine*** not mere thought. We ***experience*** knowingness through our ***hearts*** and ***souls.***

We see what happens when the world thrives on ego in pursuit of the ***love of power***. The ***new reality*** we are creating is ***Divinely*** embracing the ***power of love.***

Everyone has amazing qualities to offer. People never forget how you make them feel. ***Be unforgettable.***

Everyone makes decisions they think are best. Respecting their right to make decisions does not mean you agree. However, it is about their life not yours. Live and let live.

We co-create our reality with ***The Divine***. The essential element in the process is ***faith***. If ***we believe*** that our desire ***already exists*** it is only a matter of time and we will see it.

Now is all there ***is***. ***Now*** is the time to set sail. Make ***one*** small change ***now*** and experience a new course. ***Be*** in the ***now***. It's the ***only*** place to ***be.***

The winds soar and the tides roar. The power of ***The Universe*** flows ***through*** you and it blesses others. ***Set it free. If*** it's meant to be, ***it*** returns to thee.

Your outer world is a reflection of your inner world. Listen to your heart and dare to give your passion to a hurting planet. Fear is countered by ***faith.***

Your life is what ***you*** choose it to be. Choose to ***be*** the authentic you and be ***full-filled. Being*** fulfilled allows you to live from a ***grateful heart.***

The ***Universe*** is composed of energy as are we humans. We emit a frequency which attracts people, circumstances, etc. Love will raise your frequency. ***Be it*** and you'll ***see*** it.

A ***thought*** charged with emotion, seen in the mind's eye and believed that ***it already exists***, is the process for attracting whatever you desire.

Life can be viewed as a game, or as a dance. Every game, dance, or endeavor has rules to follow. You would typically dress in business attire for a job interview. Driving a car in traffic has rules, written and otherwise. ***The point?*** Always know the rules of what game or dance you are engaging in. This makes your participation more intentional, meaningful and ***more*** joyful.

Each of us has an ***image;*** it's the way people see us. You know you are living a life of integrity when the image others have of you is consistent with your own. The image of you that reflects in the mirror is the real you. Know thyself so you can love yourself and others.

Your thoughts can either ***create a place for you to be free***, or ***take you hostage and imprison you***. You ultimately decide based on your choices, conscious or otherwise.

Situations in life cause us to experience gratitude and sadness. Allow the sadness ***to be*** and it dissipates. The gratitude is eternal if ***you consciously*** allow it to be.

Each of us strives to be more of who we are created to be. Be not concerned with being better, just allow yourself to be ***more*** of who you are. For today only, say “I am ok just like I am right now.” When you experience ***more*** by the end of the day, life is good. You already ***are*** whole but can definitely become ***more*** if you choose.

When we have nothing to say it may be a sign to quietly listen or observe. Listen and observe that which is around you and how you feel at present. Your observations may be a source of where you choose to focus your attention.

Give the gift of ***forgiveness*** to yourself and it becomes easier to give it to others. This all season gift of ***forgiveness*** is priceless. This works best when you give unconditionally and quietly.

Right now rain is pouring down somewhere. Some rain will be absorbed into the ***earth*** and some will fall upon the bodies of water. Every single drop has a place to go and a purpose to fulfill. ***Divine providence*** (or ***nature***) handles these details effortlessly.

Truth is often difficult to handle. If it really ***is*** the truth you have been given a responsibility to walk and live in that truth. Speak not but walk in a way that you radiate truth. Love contains truth, integrity, compassion and more.

Life can be chaotic at times. Everyday should contain quiet time to consciously connect to ***The Creator***. ***Make*** time to ***be*** consciously with ***The Creator*** and you will be given more time to ***be***, ***do*** and ***have*** all you desire.

Allowing life to ***be*** complicated drains us of our ***Divinity***. Is anything so important that it complicates your life to the point that you are living beneath your ***Divinity?*** Love that is unconditional isn't complicated. ***Toxic*** relationships are.

Each of us has gifts to offer the world. We freely give away some of our gifts with no expectation of return. Some of our gifts can be converted into a hobby or a career that is a labor of love. Some gifts can be converted into a skill that provides income. Some people never give but take at every opportunity. Be discerning with regard to who and why you give, as you are giving ***Divine*** energy.

Empirical truth is fact and relative truth is based on what someone ***believes*** to be true. Relative truth might be viewed as one's opinion. This may be true for one person and not another. Most wars, misunderstandings and conflicts are based on relative truth. Therefore, live ***your*** truth and allow others to live ***theirs.*** This requires love.

The ***peace*** you experience within is directly related to your ***faith*** in ***love***. ***Hope*** is for people who temporarily waiver in faith. Walk in faith and you walk in love. Walk in love and you walk in peace. Walk in peace and you become love. Become love and all else takes care of itself.

In science two chemicals put together create something ***new***. This newly created chemical has potential the components did not have individually. Two people who come together for something, ***greater than themselves,*** also create anew. Loving co-operation will transform hearts.

When everyone who supposedly matters to you walks out on you, an interesting opportunity walks in. Depending on what you choose to call this opportunity has everything to do with its impact and value in your life. Is it loneliness or is it quiet reflection? Be grateful for serendipitous events.

Everyone allows time for the things that matter to them. If your life is busy your friends know and accept this. However, if you are ***too*** busy to allow time for friendships, you may want to re-define what ***friend*** means to you. True friendships and ***friendly*** acquaintances are completely different, as they require differing levels of care.

Feminine energy is needed to clean up the masculine messes we have on a global scale. Ladies, influence your men to love boldly and to teach that to his children, co-workers, friends and all who he encounters. Men please listen to your lady. Love is all there is, it's our salvation.

We are attracted to people who are like ourselves or those we tend to like. Birds of a feather flock together. It's familiar, predictable and requires little effort. To grow, you must go beyond ***you*** and those similar to you. Desires not yet fulfilled may require cooperation with those not yet known. Be open and they will appear.

There is a very good reason as to why we were created with ***one*** mouth and ***two*** ears. Having a mouth allows us to teach. Having ears allows us to learn. Is it any wonder that we have only one mouth and two ears? The more we are quiet and open to listening the more we learn. Be still and listen twice as often as you speak. This leads to wisdom.

Sometimes brilliant words are not on the tip of one's tongue. Sometimes they are on the tip of the tongue of a ***Higher Source*** waiting for us to be still, so ***we*** may hear.

Humans are composed of ***body, mind,*** *and* ***soul. Divine Spirit*** is in all three of those components, as we are ***Divine*** in nature. If any component of the triad is out of alignment, look to your relationship with ***Spirit.*** You will find the imbalance and the means to realign.

Many of us are wounded healers. We endured through some of life's most devastating experiences therefore we see the need to stop the bleeding. Often we learn as we go. We work through earthly issues using spiritual remedies as we are composed of spiritual energy. In the words of Earl Nightingale "when a man's world is right, the man will be right." I am perfectly imperfect, and that's ok for ***now.***

We are in a time during history that is quite unique. Our awareness has provided us the capacity to understand the power of our collective consciousness. We have the power to create a more loving reality in which to live.

I am grateful for what I see in others that sometimes frustrates me. What I see ***Is*** really me.

Each of us has unique talents and abilities that provide service to mankind. We learn our greatest lessons by engaging in service that is a labor of love. Today allow circumstances that arise to be the gateway to opportunities to be of service. A grateful heart will attract more opportunities that you can be grateful for.

Sometimes the best way to be supportive of a person is to get out of their way and allow the natural order of things to take its course. It is always best to know your own boundaries, so as to be true and honest to your own values.

Our thoughts can come from many places, situations, circumstances, senses, feelings, physical pain, etc. In a universe of order there are no accidents. There is a reason or meaning for everything and every thought. You have the power to ***choose*** which thoughts you want to discard and which thoughts deserve your attention ***now***.

There are natural laws in the physical world, such as gravity. The more you identify with the primal aspects of the physical world via the ego (safety, security, needing to be accepted, etc.) the more earth-bound and physical are your experiences. Allow the ***Divine Spirit*** within to guide you and your experiences will magically become ***Divine***.

When something happened in the past, it was ***now,*** then. When something happens in the future it will be ***now,*** then. This very moment ***is now***. Only one of the three offers you choices, opportunities, and possibilities. That is ***Now.***

People who meditate allow themselves to go into a state of ***oneness*** with the ***Divine*** and feel peaceful. It is interesting to note that people who go ***within*** rarely go ***without.***

People have goals, plans, dreams and some big ideas. However, we live in a world where time is a factor. While you wait for that perfect person to show up, or that big idea to come together, what are you doing while waiting? Is there something you love passionately, like your career, a hobby, or volunteering? ***Pour yourself into your passion!*** It will sustain you while attracting more of what you desire.

Rules are everywhere. There are social rules about who should date one another. Who says a person 4'5 can't be with someone 6'8? Who says that a man 80 can't be with a woman 45? Who says you can't eat pizza for breakfast? Who says you can't wear white after Labor Day? Who says dinner must be at 6pm? Today make note of how often you are supposed to be mindful of rules that are meaningless. ***Decide now***, to live from your authentic self.

The ***internet*** is effective for non-emotional, non-intimate communication and more. It is best used to send and receive data, when deep feelings and or heartfelt expression are not required. It is highly effective for telling people how much you appreciate, respect, and enjoy being connected to them. Kissing someone through a screen door is not the same as kissing them face to face.

Many people scurry around just to get through the day. After they sleep for the night, they start all over again. If they chose to enjoy each moment of each day their lives would be fuller, more enjoyable and more meaningful. The lesson here is to love your day as it unfolds and ***enjoy the miracles as they happen*** otherwise it's just another day.

If it is to be it is up to me. If you want ***anything*** to change ***you*** must change ***first***. ***Be the change.***

Those who lack belief in themselves call those who are visionaries, ***fools***. Those who support the ***visionaries*** in their quests call them, ***determined.*** Let no man make decisions about your heart's desire for the only true power in your heart is the ***creative wisdom*** that created you. Let that ***wisdom*** guide you always.

Look in the mirror and you see your physical self. Specifically look into your eyes and you see into your soul. The more you see into your soul a connection is created between mind and soul. This exercise enhances ***Spiritual*** strength and is an effective way to overcome your fears.

On the occasions when you don't know which way to go, go within yourself. There you will find ***the wisdom*** of ***The Universe*** in each and every cell. The answers to most of life's greatest mysteries are found there.

Letting someone into your life is not the same as letting them into your heart. Someone can exit (or be evicted) from your life and it may not affect you at all. See if you can find a judge or a high court with enough power to evict someone from your heart.

Everyone makes decisions they think are best. Respecting their right to make decisions does not mean you agree. It is about their life not yours. Live and let live.

For a few moments right now, ***be*** still and listen, you will be guided effortlessly to where you need to be.

Everyone deserves happiness to the extent that they believe they are worthy of having it. Beliefs are mindsets which we consciously or sub-consciously adopt. Consciously choose to believe you deserve happiness by doing something to affirm that belief. An example is do something good for yourself and allow yourself to accept it. This is how to condition one's self into a new mindset.

A belief is basically what you hold to be true and may not vibrate as true for others. Each of us is an expression of the ***creative wisdom*** from whence we came. That is true for all of us. Just for today, treat everyone as though they are a long lost brother or sister. See what that does for the way ***you*** feel about yourself.

They ***only*** thing that makes today different, is the way you rise to the occasion to be of service to ***your Creator***, ***yourself***, and your neighbor. The rest is mere details.

Reasonable people are more likely to conform to whatever they are told even when what they are told is unreasonable. The greatest inventions, discoveries and theories are brought to light by those who are unreasonable in relation to the norm. Reasonable choices are usually safer but less rewarding. Want to find your purpose, passion, and bliss? ***Be unreasonable.***

It is easy to complain about something that you don't like. Complaining about something usually causes it to grow bigger, not better. Just for today, whenever something bothers you, do one small thing to ***be the solution***. Complaints are grounded in powerlessness. Solutions are grounded in infinite possibilities.

The person who views life as a sea of infinite possibilities is powerful beyond measure. Whereas, the person who views life as ***it must be this specific way*** is ***powerless*** beyond measure. It's your world; create it as you ***see*** it.

We are each unique. We each want to be known but may want to hide at the same time. We each want to be loved but sometimes have fears. This paradoxical mindset is one of the causes of mixed signals. When we ***learn to know and love ourselves we can then know and love others***.

Many people say what they believe others want to hear. If you really care about someone tell them what you think and/or how you feel. Speaking from the heart may be difficult at times but you will never regret being true to yourself. ***Now*** is a great time to start.

Strong character and charm may be in your genealogy but they are developed within each moment based on the ***values you presently hold***. We live our values.

As we begin to awaken to ***Divine consciousness*** we take on a responsibility. We are to share it with others by ***being*** an example of what is possible.

The word ***want*** denotes that you do not ***have*** and is associated with lack. The word ***desire*** is stronger and often associated with ***a burning within the soul***. If you ***desire*** someone or something in your life, display actions that request ***The Universe*** work with you. Requests based on love and gratitude gets ***Divine*** attention more rapidly.

Sometimes the quietest person is much more interesting than the loudest person. Look at the quiet people around you and open a conversation. You might just find that they have a lot to say if given the chance.

Want fulfillment and happiness? ***Allow*** yourself to ***be*** yourself. No one is more qualified to be you than ***you***. You are unique and worthy and have a lot to share.

If you catch a glimpse of heaven on ***earth*** you ***are*** blessed more than most and have the power to create it again. If you have to yet to experience this, associate with those that have; it too will be yours.

The ***world*** can only benefit from your magnificent contribution once you acknowledge that you ***are*** magnificence and accept responsibility for sharing it.

People create loving families. Loving families create community. Communities create cities/states/provinces which, in turn create countries of the world. The ***world*** can only be peaceful if loving values are rooted in ***its people***. ***We*** are ***the people*** so let it begin with ***us.*** Just for ***today*** show kindness and compassion to every living creature.

Every person is created as an integral part of humanity and at the same time is a unique creation. As parts of humanity we rely on other parts, similar to an automobile needing an engine, tires, fuel, etc. ***Be*** your best and assist others to be their best, the ride is much smoother.

Past and ***future*** are reference points that do not presently exist. The ***present*** has scents, sounds, sights, tastes and people to love. The ***present*** is ***yours now.***

When we hear sounds like cars horns, rain, thunder, etc. we know exactly what it is. However, when we hear words spoken to us in conversation we tend to hear exactly what we ***want*** to hear. Listen to what people are ***really*** saying.

Many people believe that ***love*** is an emotion. Joy is an emotion, as is sadness. ***Love*** is: ***intentional, decisive, evolving action.*** Commit to actions that express love.

It is wonderful to have nice things like money, houses, jewelry and ***stuff*** in general. Your stuff can not kiss you, hug you, or tell you look nice today. A truly rich life is about who you have in your life, not what you have.

Everyone has things that make them unique, such as skills, traits, abilities, etc. Some of the gifts they possess are not readily detectable by everyone. Today, be observant when in the presence of others; find one of the things that makes them the unique creation they are.

An idea without energy is like a car without fuel. Passion is the fuel that allows an idea to take flight. You must be absolutely committed to this idea and envision ***it as so.*** Your emotional feelings about this vision are what fuel the ***Intention***. An attitude of ***Gratitude*** paves the way.

Everything begins with ***an idea***. It doesn't have to make sense to be worthwhile. It only requires that you are passionately committed to ***intending*** this idea to become reality. The first step is to give the idea your focused attention. This creates connection between it and you.

Be expectant and you will attract things into your life. Having unspecific expectations doesn't allow ***The Universe*** to assist you. Going it alone may lead to many disappointments. Choose co-operation.

Be open to what this day brings. You may already have plans. As you go about your day, signs may appear guiding you to slightly alter your plans. Remember, our realities are co-creations in conjunction with ***Our Creator***. When a sign shows up ***The Creator*** is giving input. All we need is faith. Magical manifestations may appear before your eyes.

Look at the values and character of five people with whom you spend the most time. Do they inspire you? Do they make suggestions that enhance your life? Are their behaviors and habits something you find appealing? By being in your life do they inspire you to want to grow as a person? Use wisdom to choose those that surround you.

We use words to communicate, describe and show affection. Sometimes we even say hurtful things. There is a saying, "***talk is cheap***." It's cheap because it costs us nothing to speak. Action requires energy and demonstrates how we feel. Be clear with words and ***loving*** with actions.

Situations in life cause us to experience gratitude and sadness. Allow the sadness ***to be*** and it soon dissipates. The gratitude is eternal, if ***you*** allow it to be.

Perceptions are based on our beliefs, as this is how we filter our perceptions. Beliefs should hold up under your own unbiased scrutiny, even if new information becomes available. Examining what we believe requires analysis that few are willing to explore. Thus denial and illusion are more common than ***authentic living.***

The antidote to overcome fear is faith. Faith is what gives us the courage to take action in spite of fear.

Every relationship; friends, lovers, spouses, etc. is but another connection to ***The Divine.*** The egotistical nature of some human beings usually leads to relationships failing. We become fearful or unsure that we won't stay loved then our ego goes into safety mode. The cure for fear is love. Sometimes the best way to love is to get out of the way.

Certain behavior upsets us. We see behavior in others that reflects aspects of ourselves. When the other person acts out, be compassionate. By showing compassion to them you show compassion to yourself. Both parties can start healing based on this one act.

Everyone has tasks that are pending. It could be as simple as filling out a warranty card and mailing it. Imagine how much energy you have given to thinking about such tasks. Today when you complete a task do ***one*** small additional thing that may otherwise cause energy draining thoughts.

Every person is similar to a single facet of a perfect diamond. A diamond has many facets and each plays a part in bringing forth the beauty of the total gemstone. You are a facet of a much greater diamond and all you must do is shine on brightly. ***Be*** the unique facet that you are.

The ***mind*** thinks, chooses what to believe and retains facts. True ***knowing*** is the realm of ***Spirit*** not thought. We ***feel*** it through the experiences within our ***hearts & souls.***

It is often difficult to challenge what we have been taught to believe. Most people go through life without questioning what they were taught. An unchallenged belief that causes you grief ultimately controls you.

People often search for answers to life's mysteries. You have a body, mind and soul that might need healing with ***Spirit energy***. Learn to ***love, heal, understand***, and ***radiate*** goodness from within and you will have total health.

People enter and exit our lives for reasons. We don't always know why. If we accept it as a blessing or a learning experience we can view every connection as being worthwhile. When someone doesn't quite fit into our lives (or vice versa) we should ***bless them and let them be***. This is how we honor them for passing through with gratitude.

Going with ***the flow*** is being in ***Divine momentum*** as you are in alignment with ***The Universe***. Allow ***the flow*** to prevail and attract ***serendipitous*** experiences. Serendipity is when unexpected good fortune presents itself, simply because you are in ***the flow***.

There are times when we feel alone, even abandoned. It has been proven that each of us, our planet and our ***Creator*** are energetically connected as ***one***. If you are alone use your mind to bring whomever you want into your space. Talk to them, ask questions and engage them. You are already connected. Call them and they will appear.

You will discover your greatest traits, unique gifts and inner strengths when you view adversity as opportunity. A feeling of ***job well done*** goes to those who create solutions that serve others. Anyone can be a problem finder. See things differently and responsibly create of solutions.

To thy own self ***be*** true. Be true to ***your*** dreams, beliefs, feelings and ***vision*** of what is possible. Your life has to be some way, so it may as well be ***your*** way. A ***vision***, a ***plan*** and ***means*** of ***measuring progress*** is all you need.

Your future is only as clear as you are. Do you know what you desire in life? Are you willing to ***exchange*** your time, money and resources to have or experience what you want? ***The Creator*** is all about loving balance. We co-create our future with ***The Creator***, not alone. Your future is now.

Today, look at every situation and every person that you encounter as being ***perfect***. Speak less than usual and listen more intently than usual. Be aware of the ***signs*** with which ***The Universe*** guides you. Every person, place, or thing has a message for you; just accept it for what it is.

Most people never ask, "***What is truly important to me***?" Most react to their immediate circumstances, rather than asking the question. Do yourself a favor, ask.

Have you given away authority over your thoughts and dreams to some outside group or person? We are created with ***Infinite Intelligence*** residing within us. Call this ***Divine Source,*** or by whatever name you like. It is the authority within and guides accordingly if we allow.

Relationships are like business contracts with terms and conditions. People mistakenly believe that certain things are implied when, in fact, never agreed to. Be clear with your communication so as to be true to your ***intentions***.

The left side of your brain and the right side of your brain are parts of the same organism called the body. ***We***, you and ***I*** are parts of the same ***human species body*** and are connected. ***We*** are ***one.*** Today, treat others in a manner that says ***you are me and I am you and we are one.***

Today is the day that you get to make that ***one decision*** that will change the course of your life. Remember, this illusive butterfly we call the future is actually created with today's decisions. ***One decision*** you make can be of monumental importance, it can change ***everything***.

Life is not about past or future. It is about the way we manage the moment. Treat this moment as though it is the only moment that exists. This moment reveals a new ***Now***.

If we had not made our so-called mistakes we would not be the people we are today. Well intentioned people do things that may be out of alignment because they don't ***see*** the misalignment. Allowing others to grow without interference is truly an act of love.

Have you ever thought about someone, the phone rings, and it's them? Ever have a thought and the person you are talking to expresses the exact thought as you? Ever had something on your mind and the answer shows up from the most unlikely place? We are all connected and the power to summon up this energy is within us all. We are ***one*** with ***The Creator***. Share your power; be valuable to others.

The only reason you know how old you are, is because you were told what year you were born. If you had no clue as to when you were born, age would not matter. Cultivate and embrace the spiritual you and it becomes unimportant. See yourself as timeless as you are composed of ***Divine*** energy ***that*** never dies.

Everyone has a choice as to how they start their day. It may start with thanks, prayer or meditation, pondering over coffee or tea, planning the day or mere silence. The way you start your day sets the tone of the day. It's your choice to start when you arise, or start over when needed.

You were created for one thing. That is to learn the experience of ***love.*** Those who suffer are often unaware of this. The ***Creator*** did not create us to experience suffering.

Everyone desires ***inspiration, intelligence*** and ***meaningful*** interaction. We seek it in the most unusual places, whether on a plane or in an elevator. The electricity of ***The Universe*** keeps us moving. Seek your electricity from sources that ***empower you*** and make you feel good.

There is a reason why ***life*** doesn't come with an instruction manual. The manual would be obsolete before you finished reading it. Life often changes, so play it as you see fit.

We never know who is listening to us or who is observing our actions. We are ***spirit energy*** beings. We energetically change whatever environment we enter. If your energy is empowering and loving you will bring empowerment and love to your environment. Be mindful of your power.

Just for today, do one thing that you have been avoiding. If it is a task that is boring, make it interesting. If it is something laborious, make it a labor of love. ***Changing the way you look at the situation alters the final outcome***.

If you are searching for something, your thoughts and actions demonstrate that you are missing something. If you search for someone to love, your actions show that you are unloved. If you are a loving person you will attract people who will ***exchange in kind*** (love in this case) with you. ***Be*** that which you seek to attract.

Life is amazing when we ***supposedly*** run out of ideas or resources. If we go within and tap into our ***higher self,*** new ideas and resources appear in abundance. All it takes is a trip inward to change things outward. ***You*** are the world.

Be grateful for the many small things in life and realize that sometimes we take them for granted. Many moments make a life. ***This*** moment is the most important.

Sometimes we ***must*** go outside of our comfort zone to convey our truth to another human being. The price we pay may be rejection, embarrassment or showing vulnerability. If we choose to keep our truth a secret we run the risk of experiencing inner turmoil. Turmoil causes stress. It has been proven that stress is the source of all disease.

Everything is created with ***Universal*** intelligence; therefore ***The Creator*** resides in all things. When speaking to another person, you are speaking to ***The Creator***. When petting an animal you are touching ***The Creator***. When looking in the mirror ***The Creator*** is there. The kingdom of heaven ***is*** within. You are never alone.

We are in human form for many years; however we are always of the spirit. Human rights focus on our physical selves and how we are treated by governments, etc. How would this world look if we focused on ***spiritual rights*** which are sovereign rights bestowed on us by our ***Creator?***

A ***new era*** takes on a life of its own. The ***future*** is created in the ***present***. Envision yourself ***being, doing and having*** your best, ***now***. We create our life in ***this present*** moment. Step back and witness ***this*** moment. ***Now*** is where all possibilities exist.

At the beginning of a New Year resolutions are often made. ***Today*** is all that really exists. A New Year usually generates thoughts that ***things will be better***. ***Now*** is where you make tomorrow better. ***Now*** is where you make changes rather than resolutions. Say ***yes*** to ***Now.***

Look at something from the side and it looks a certain way. Look at it on a slight angle and it looks slightly different. You may see beauty that wasn't otherwise visible. There is much beauty if we see through the eyes of ***The Creator***.

Some people confuse their beliefs with what they know to be true. What you know can be proven on some level, if only to yourself. What you believe is a ***belief*** not a fact. Put your beliefs to the test of ***experiencing what you believe***. An experience leaves evidence such as; memories, feelings and footprints. This becomes what you now ***know.***

People may say anything they want about someone else. If you ***live by standards that you set***; what others say or think becomes unimportant. Define your personal standards and your path will always be lit by the light that is you.

Friends show up at different stages of our lives. Some friends are always there and some show up once in a while. ***Be*** memorable by ***being*** friendly to everyone.

There is risk involved in living true to your heart and soul. Some people will walk away and leave your life. There is also risk involved in living according to someone else's rule book. Ponder this question silently to yourself. Which of these is more in alignment with my ***Divine*** nature?

Imagination is the workshop of the mind. Everyone can imagine things that have not been invented. Give your past memories a rest and allow your imagination to create fresh new experiences. Your imagination creates images and those images become your future which is created, ***now.***

The past is not a place but a memory. The experiences it brought are now known. The future is not a place but an idea of where ***today*** is taking us. Envision ***today*** the way you see your future as ***being***. ***Be it*** and you ***See it***.

Every ending is a new beginning. New beginnings are proof that we never die but begin anew. ***Love*** is the glue that holds creation together. Fear is the opposite of ***love***. Anything less than ***love*** is an illusion, ***Be love.***

Our ego leads us to believe that what we desire is in short supply. We fearfully set about to acquire that which we ***think*** is scarce. Love is all there is and therefore there is no scarcity. Your heart is your guide to discern ego from ***love.***

Your power goes far beyond your physical self. Connect with someone in need and see how powerful you really are. You will empower them at the same time. That is what this invisible connection called ***oneness*** is all about.

This very moment in your life has all the potential of any other moment. You are love and loved right now. You may desire to hit a ball out of the park. The ball is right in front of you. Enjoy the swing; the rest takes care of itself.

Everyone knows ***present*** means ***here*** and ***now***. Past is a memory, not a physical place. We utilize the past for learning, reference, and commemorative purposes. It's ok to look back, but rarely does it work if we go back. There's no place like home. Home is where your heart is ***now***.

Your values determine your standards regarding what you will and will not accept in life. Veer from your standards and you may feel regret. If you live by your standards, you are living true to yourself. Nobody ever said ***being true to thy self*** was going to be easy.

New friends may see ***potential*** in us that we do not. ***Potential*** is a creative power that is ever present. Doors will open when we are willing to use our ***potential*** to explore new possibilities.

Sometimes we ***do things*** and later ***undo*** them. Either way, the same level of care must be rendered. That level of care should be employed while in, out, or in between.

What determines the fulfillment and passion in your life? People allow circumstances and others expectations to influence how they live. If you want to play it safe and never get hurt, then sit on the sidelines. The game of life is played ***in the (quantum) field,*** not on the sidelines.

Stop whatever it is you are doing and take a deep breath. Allow yourself the opportunity to see, smell, hear, taste and touch whatever is present. In so doing, you stop ***being busy*** and are just ***being***. ***Being*** allows peace to be ever-present and attracts love as a benefit.

You may have heard it said, "***It's your world***." If your eyes are open to the world in front of you, you may see a panoramic view that leaves you awe struck. If a curtain is hiding the view, you will see things differently. The difference between the two views and the possibilities each holds depends on which way the draw string is pulled.

Now is all that exists. Yesterday may have existed but does not exist ***now***. Tomorrow may be anticipated but does not exist ***now***. The ***present*** is all that exists.

Your present ***level of awareness*** determines the extent to which you experience gratitude. Today be more aware.

Thinking that something could be a certain way requires an open mind. ***Believing*** it could be requires ***faith. Knowing*** that it exists before it is physically created requires ***vision***.

A specific situation may present you with a question. ***The Universe*** often leaves out words but presents us with a picture. Be open to receiving the answers you seek from whatever source ***The Universe*** provides.

If someone appears to be undermining us, it is kind to give them the benefit of the doubt when confronting them. If they choose to not take the high road, ***we must do what is necessary*** to ***take care of ourselves*** appropriately.

Life is not measured by how many people ***you*** love. It is measured by how many people know ***you*** and love you, faults and all. To be known and loved simultaneously is the most meaningful love.

It is said by many; "***All men are created equal***." This refers to ***The Creator*** creating us with equal love and gifts.

It is the responsibility of each person to discover their gifts and glorify ***The Creator*** through ***co-operative contribution.***

Your life is based on what ***you*** put your energy into. Focus on what you do not have, and you will experience lack. Focus on worry and you will attract more to worry about. ***You*** are the author of your life. Write it like a fairy tale.

If all aspects of your future were known, the mystique and fun would be removed. Be thankful you don't know every detail, for the lessons that inevitably come your way would have less value. The object is to play the hand you've been dealt, with your highest level of ***awareness*** and excellence.

You ***are*** perfect ***now*** as you are a creation of ***The Divine*** and therefore embody ***The Divine***. Be conscious of this divinity and your world magically transforms.

Self respect is the basis for all relationships. It extends even further but this initial awareness puts things into perspective. Developing and living by one's own personal standards is where self respect begins. ***Know thyself***.

When being truly conscious of taking care of myself a different quality of people flow into my life. They are of a higher vibration. My vibration determines who I attract.

In some way, each person gives to others. Today, give a bit more with no expectation of additional return. Consider doing it just because you want to. Your sincere intention will also tell ***The Universe*** that you are grateful. Then ***The Universe*** will send more to be grateful for.

Three things differ from the physical to the metaphysical. The physical has form, time and space. The metaphysical realm does not. Earthly relationships are relative to form time and space. ***Be*** in ***the Now*** and ***love what is.***

Some of your strength is found within your fears. Fear is experienced in the body as well as the mind. Many think courage is the opposite of fear. Courage is the ability to take action ***through*** the fear. The ***opposite of fear is faith***. Have faith and you will have the courage you need.

We are being shown ways to ascend our physical selves and become more of the ***Spirit beings*** that we truly are. Spirituality is interesting, enlightening, fulfilling, and ***fun***. Nowhere in the equation is ***serious*** to be found.

Every person has a gift or a message to convey to the world. Once you know what message you are to deliver, you must ***live it while you give it.*** Integrity is a lifestyle.

People come and go. It can be painful to see someone go. The passing of time often reveals that they were not an ***appropriate fit.*** Their leaving may have saved us from even greater disappointment and thus is the real blessing.

Many situations in life call for extraordinary measures. Important situations often call for more than thinking; they require us to analyze how we ***feel***. Our emotional feelings let us know if we are in alignment with ***Divine*** flow, or are we being resistant. That which we resist, persists!

Each of us is given a writing tablet and a writing instrument when we are born. We can intentionally write our own destiny. If we choose to do otherwise our destiny will be written by chance and circumstance. When a block of marble was placed before Michelangelo, he saw David. Look in the mirror and you will see ***your destiny***.

You do not have to be religious or have any belief system to gain insight from faith based teachers. The Dalai Lama teaches that his religion is simple. It is ***kindness.***

We are all connected through ***The Universe***. What we do to each other we do to ourselves. Asking for what we desire is a way to take care of ourselves. We can then also take care of the unfortunate. If more of us are ***forgiving***, the unfortunate will become fewer.

I am grateful for what I see in others that sometimes frustrates me. What I see is a version of ***me***.

The shortest distance between two points is a straight line. Therefore, the shortest distance to work around something is to work straight ***through it***. It is not always the easiest way but ultimately it is the ***only*** method that works.

When it comes to any undertaking the best place to start is ***here and now***. If it turns out there is a better place to start; by the time you realize it, you will be ***here.***

Each of us has beliefs about many things. Our beliefs shape our values. Our values form our character and show up in our behavior. Our behavior is our beliefs in action. Our beliefs about ***what is possible*** create our reality. Create a new reality by creating a new belief.

There are many definitions for ***love***. The dictionary reads; ***love is*** affectionate concern for another. The opposite is, not hate but indifference. A smile given to a poor person is nice but will that feed him? ***Love is*** an ***action.***

When someone asks ***"how are you"*** they are not really asking ***"tell me how you feel"*** and wanting a response. The next time someone asks, answer as a way of expressing what you are grateful for in that moment. If nothing comes to mind say; ***"better and better, thank you for asking."***

The Universe has its own flow, like a river. Just for today, allow yourself to surrender to ***Universal*** flow. You will be amazed at what shows up when ***The Universe*** does ***its*** thing. Opportunities and experiences abound if you allow.

Sometimes your wants and desires are very much heartfelt. Your mind may want to argue with your heart. Your mind may keep you safe but following your heart is way more in tune with ***The Universe***.

You can be in any moment you choose; past, present, or future. Past and future are mere illusions. Only ***now*** truly exists. Choose an illusion or choose ***now.*** It's your choice.

Many people have premonitions in dreams and they come true. Does that mean the future already exists and they traveled there in their sleep, or, have they created reality? Maybe dreaming of those things actually created them.

We possess the capability to be truly ***authentic*** but it takes courage. The more ***authentic*** we ***are*** the more we ***attract*** people who are ***authentic***. To have peace, ***be*** peace. To have joy, ***be*** joy. To have love, ***be*** love.

The world you experience outside of you is a mirror of what you experience inside. If you want to experience things differently outside, things inside must change first. It begins with a ***burning desire to which you are committed***. It is a state of ***being***. ***Be*** it and you ***see*** it.

Do you live in a state of ***hope*** or a state of ***faith***? Hope is a future concept that may never come to ***be***. ***Faith*** is a state of ***being, now.*** True ***faith*** is felt in the heart. You are a ***Divine creation.*** Have faith and ***The Divine provides***.

The term ***love*** is frequently misinterpreted and puzzles many people. For ***now*** allow yourself to ***be*** in a state of ***gratitude*** for one thing you care about, you ***will*** experience love from ***within.***

We are born with unlimited potential. We are ***taught*** limitation and ***told*** who we ***are***. When we shed that which is out of resonance with ***truth***, we reclaim our ***true self.***

Words that are disempowering are found throughout our daily speech. Today, remove ***don't, no, can't*** and replace them with different empowering word patterns.

In our ***Universe*** where balance is a ***Universal*** law the most unlikely pairings create perfect balance. When we surrender and see with the ***Spirit within*** balance finds us.

Today is the ***only*** day of your life, as it is all that exists. With that thought in mind are you approaching your day more ***intentionally?*** If not, why?

We are ***body, mind, and soul.*** All three have needs and the soul and heart have desires. ***Focused attention*** determines the level of fulfillment you experience.

Forgiveness is for us, not the other person. When we allow ourselves to forgive we find gratitude for an otherwise unpleasant experience. ***Forgive*** and ***forget.***

Do I live ***in*** the moment or ***for*** the moment? ***For*** the moment may bring painful consequences. ***In*** the moment ***is the joy of being*** through ***intentional consciousness.***

Only you have the unique qualities that are you. Down to your fingerprints everything about you is unique. ***Be*** the unique ***being*** you are created to be.

Just for today, ***be*** in a ***mindset*** that compels you to ***do*** something you've been resisting. Go outside your comfort zone. Allow yourself to ***have faith*** to triumph over fears.

What we do tomorrow is of no importance as tomorrow does not exist, today. What we do in ***this*** moment affects all of our tomorrows. ***Now*** is eternal.

We attract who we are, ***not*** who we want. ***Be*** a match for what you want by shifting your consciousness into ***being the best version of you.***

The way you feel emotionally determines what you experience. The more heartfelt your feelings the more vivid your world is. Pay ***love*** and ***gratitude forward.***

In a ***Universe*** where abundance is a birthright some settle for suffering. You have a choice to be a victim or ***the victor***. ***Be*** victorious living from your heart.

Gratitude is a state of ***being***. Choosing to ***be*** grateful raises your vibration, then more is attracted to be grateful for. You have been blessed in this special way, so ***just be it.***

Gratitude for anything (clean water, sunshine, etc.) immediately shifts your awareness and realigns your attitude toward all things. ***Allow*** gratitude to prevail.

Words are powerful. They have meaning, energetic power, and the ***Intention*** we put behind them. Pay close attention to your words. Do your words empower you and others?

Thoughts, words, and feelings are the means by which we ***attract*** everything. Focused attention is where vibrational energy flows. Be ***mindful*** as to what you ***focus*** upon.

The Universe is conscious love. Love from your heart consciously and be ***one*** with ***The Universe***. You will attract more conscious love into your relationships.

In Physics, for every action there is an equal and opposite reaction. For every action (when you are conscious) there should be a ***loving response*** rather than a reaction.

Being all you are capable of being is directly proportionate to your awareness at a soul level. The soul seeks to influence the mind but sometimes the ego part of the mind gets in the way. Train your ego to serve you.

Your level of perfection is good enough to start attracting your heart's desire. The perfect time is ***now***! Name ***it*** and claim ***it*** and have gratitude that you created it.

Denial is a fear based state of mind that resists what is possible. Your possibilities are unlimited. Now is the time to say yes to this power that is within you and is ***Divine***.

If you say what's in your heart, you don't have to worry about what's on your mind.

Life can get busy and the most important people may get put on the side because you are so busy. You ***take*** time to see clients but sometimes you must ***make*** (create) time for who and what is most important in your life.

The little ***go wrongs*** of each day can be viewed as challenges or opportunities. It depends on how you choose to see things. Be open to change. It's inevitable.

Life is not a game of winners and losers. It is an experience of ***Divine*** expression. The happiest people lead fulfilling rather than satisfying lives. Happiness is a byproduct of fulfillment; a byproduct of living on ***purpose***.

The dictionary shows motivation and inspiration as being the same. Not necessarily so. Motivation fuels the desire to run that last lap while ***inspiration*** fuels the desire to be and do something you are passionate about. After you get motivated to run that last lap you will be tired. When you engage in actions fueled by ***inspiration*** you will rejuvenate.

Heed messages of ***inner wisdom***, they always speak ***truth***.

If life is to have meaning you will have to take risks. The great motivational speaker Earl Nightingale once said; ***"Conformity makes cowards of us all."*** Conforming is being and doing the same as everyone else. This is not a genuine expression of your true self. Know yourself and proceed in accordance with your heart and soul.

Faith is what you believe to be true, not a universal fact. Your faith (even when others think you are crazy) will guide you to overcome any obstacle if ***passion*** fuels your faith. Your quality of your life is equal to your passion.

Life is not about our past or our future. It is about ***the way we manage the moment***. Treat this moment as though it is the only moment. This moment reveals a new ***Now***.

To get things accomplished we need to have a reason or a ***why***. If you ask out loud; ***"Why must I get this done,"*** you will come up a motivating factor. Sometimes motivation is not enough to get us moving. That is when ***Inspiration*** is desired. What feelings inspire you to take action?

Why, is the most important question you can ask yourself. ***How,*** (when it appears impossible) is the realm of ***The Divine***. If you ask ***The Divine*** you will be shown a way, then ***how,*** is no longer an issue. It just works that way.

Everyone has their place in this world. We create ***our place*** by creating circumstances that attract a resonating truth. Personal belief systems (no matter what the belief is) are amazingly powerful. What you see in ***your*** world is a direct reflection of the thoughts you believe to be true.

The ***inner*** you is who you really are. The ***outward*** you is who you allow the public to see based on what you reveal about yourself. Everyone has the ability to live authentically and be true to their ***inner*** self. If you really want to experience connection to others, ***be the inner you***.

People have opinions about you, even if they claim to be non-judgmental. Their opinions are based on their perception of you. What ***you*** think of ***yourself*** has everything to do with what you believe about yourself. Ponder three qualities about yourself that you really love. Then take three minutes to express gratitude for them.

This moment, and everything about it; the surroundings, sounds, people, thoughts and feelings will never be exactly like this ever again. Whenever possible it is important to acknowledge the uniqueness of ***Now.***

To achieve a new result something different must be done. Just for today, rather than focus on yourself, find one needy person and give them five dollars. Be sure you feel good about doing it. ***Someone hurts more than you***.

Your intuition (some call it a gut feeling) sends signals about what feels right or wrong to you. It is not based on logic but on feelings triggered by the ***higher self*** within.

Your intuition does not tell the future. Just like your mind, your intuition can change, as it knows no time.

Be truthful, real and forthright. These things will mirror back the answers to life's riddles. All you have to do is ***be.***

Beliefs are what we choose to treat as ***the truth***. People believe different things therefore we develop different personal values. If your beliefs about something don't feel right, you can always change what you believe. That is the secret to evolving and growing as a person.

Your perception of life is a reality that you create. If you allow circumstances, outside influences or logic to keep you from realizing your dreams, you will create a corresponding reality. On the other hand, being a dreamer of action requires you to be ***unreasonable***. We were taught to be reasonable, not creative. DaVinci was ***unreasonable***.

Your first thought upon awakening is on your mind for a reason. You are holding that thought as a reminder to do something or address an issue. ***Allow*** that awakening thought to take flight. It may take you to a beautiful place.

Today, you have the opportunity to change the world. Smile and show people that you care. Help someone or do something different than usual to be kind. Your ***intended*** actions will have a ripple effect and the vibration expands.

Do you want to be happy or do you want to be right? If you want to be happy even though you may be right, being right doesn't matter, does it?

The love you experience in life is ***not*** necessarily equal to the love in your heart. The love you experience is in direct proportion to the amount of and risks you take. There are no returns, no guarantees, or money back. ***Trust yourself.***

Gratitude is one of the most powerful states of being as it comes from a humble, loving place. When we show ***gratitude*** we give off a specific vibration. The vibration of ***gratitude*** brings us more for which we can be grateful.

Ideas without energy are like cars without fuel. Passionate commitment is required. You must be passionate about this idea and ***see it as so***. The feeling of ***seeing it as so*** is what fuels the ***Intention; Gratitude*** expedites its fulfillment.

Everything begins with ***an idea***. It may seem like a day dream but an idea none the less. It doesn't have to make sense to be worthy but does require that you are passionately committed to ***Intending*** this idea into reality.

Today is the day to see something wonderful in the most unusual places. Beauty, grace, elegance and precision are all around us and within us. ***Discover*** along today's path.

The solution to all problems is: ***give love to all and receive love from all.*** Governments, institutions and business rarely make a difference. People are who effect change by helping their fellow man and woman.

Each of us has an ***ego*** that is designed to serve as a survival mechanism. If you use your ***ego*** and not allow it to use you; you will create loving possibilities that connect you to others. Separateness is an illusion and ***ego*** keeps us in illusion. Live what you love; ***release egotistical illusions***.

Look at pictures taken over the last three years. Look at your surroundings and the people in the photos. Then, ponder ***who was in your life*** during that time. You attracted them. Their values ***reflect your state of being***.

You have the ***right to question anything*** that does not resonate as truth. Be your own authority when seeking the truth. ***You have the power*** to validate your feelings of what does and what does not resonate as true for you

Life is not about our past or our future. It is about ***the way we manage the moment.*** Treat this moment as though it is the ***only*** moment that exists. This moment reveals a new ***Now***. You can find meaning in this new moment.

Knowledge is gained through education and experience. Wisdom is gained through experience. A person's true level of knowledge may be subjective, but wisdom speaks for itself and resonates truth in a powerful way.

It is well researched that people want to feel worthy and to be loved. It is best to ask questions rather than assume. Disappointing answers are better than self created illusions.

Each of us encounter people in our lives; relatives, friends, co-workers, neighbors and strangers. When you have contact with people, your sphere (or circle so to speak) connects with theirs. If it feels good ***say thank you***. If not, ***silently say thank you for experiencing all that is***.

Sometimes our plans go perfect, other times, plans fall through or change. When a plan is cancelled or changed, view this as ***attracting an alternative opportunity.*** If plans had gone accordingly, this opportunity would not exist.

Consider changing your mind about ***one thing*** today. You decide what to change your mind about. Whatever that one thing is; do it just for today. Consider ***trying on this idea*** whenever your present mindset does not serve you well.

We sometimes overlook the little things in life and focus on grand ideas. Be mindful that ***kindness*** toward people and sincere compliments may change someone's outlook. Use a calm tone of voice when dealing with issues. Smile at someone who isn't smiling. ***Small things add up***.

Actions tend to reveal people's character. It's important to consider ***Intention and Influence.*** Some people's values are influenced without their knowledge. Media, pop culture and educational institutions influence us. Consider ***exactly what you allow*** into your family's awareness.

Knowledge comes from within and the outside world. It can be used by the one who learns it or it ***can be shared***. Freely give what you have learned to whoever needs or wants it. ***Giving transforms the giver and the receiver***.

World peace is exemplary to strive for. However, ***peace begins within*** each of us first. Make today a day of being peaceful within yourself and in your world. Do whatever it takes today to love yourself and those around you. If anything gets in the way, ***remind yourself to be peaceful***.

Once upon a time everything you now see did not exist. Technology is not limited unless our thinking is. The world needs our help. Our children deserve to a world that is friendly, loving and beautiful. ***Be the change you seek.***

People play games in business, personal relationships and often when raising children. Today, start viewing life as a dance not a game. Games breed competition, which can become divisive. Dance requires ***co-operation,*** and breeds harmonious thought and action. ***Today, I dance.***

The true test of our character is not measured by the moments we have prepared for but rather, the unforeseen. For some, adversity is a motivator that allows their best traits to emerge. For others, adversity presents obstacles. Be your best, as adversities are a natural part of life.

My Emergence Journal

My Emergence Journal

My Emergence Journal

My Emergence Journal

My Emergence Journal

My Emergence Journal

My Emergence Journal

My Emergence Journal

My Emergence Journal

My Emergence Journal

My Emergence Journal

My Emergence Journal

My Emergence Journal

My Emergence Journal

My Emergence Journal

My Emergence Journal

My Emergence Journal

My Emergence Journal

My Emergence Journal

My Emergence Journal

My Emergence Journal

My Emergence Journal

My Emergence Journal

My Emergence Journal

My Emergence Journal

My Emergence Journal

My Emergence Journal

My Emergence Journal

My Emergence Journal

My Emergence Journal

My Emergence Journal

My Emergence Journal

My Emergence Journal

My Emergence Journal

My Emergence Journal

My Emergence Journal

My Emergence Journal

My Emergence Journal

My Emergence Journal

My Emergence Journal

My Emergence Journal

My Emergence Journal

My Emergence Journal

My Emergence Journal

My Emergence Journal

My Emergence Journal

My Emergence Journal

My Emergence Journal

My Emergence Journal

Topic References

Quantum Physics and Metaphysics

2, 3, 5, 7, 8, 9, 12, 15, 17, 18, 19, 20, 21, 24, 26, 27, 28, 30, 32, 33, 35, 38, 41, 42, 43, 44, 45, 46, 47, 49, 50, 54, 57, 58, 59, 62, 63, 64, 65, 66, 67, 68

Law of Attraction

1, 2, 6, 7, 10, 14, 16, 17, 19, 20, 23, 29, 38, 39, 46, 53, 58, 60, 61, 62, 64, 67, 68

Responsibility and Accountability

4, 5, 6, 7, 8, 9, 10, 11, 12, 13, 14, 15, 16, 17, 18, 24, 29, 32, 35, 36, 42, 45, 47, 48, 50, 51, 52, 53, 55, 56, 60, 61, 62

CPSIA information can be obtained at www.ICGtesting.com
227889LV00001B/16/P

9 781608 446230